DEBRIS

LEWIS DEFOREST BROWN

debris

Lewis DeForest Brown

Ithuriel's Spear
San Francisco

Copyright © 2010 by Lewis De Forest Brown.

Cover and book design by Plainfeather Printworks.

Front cover photo: "The Eagle Nebula" Credit: NASA, ESO and the Hubble Heritage team (STScI/AURA).
Back cover portrait of the author by Adra Anne Brown.
All rights reserved.

ISBN 978-0-9793390-7-3
Library of Congress Control Number: 2010932495
Ithuriel's Spear is a fiscally sponsored project of Intersection for the Arts, San Francisco.

www.ithuriel.com

Dedicated to Bernadette Semple Barberini

I am a member of the orchestra.
I am not the orchestra.
Whatever I play is a contribution.
The sound you hear is what I hear.

I am the poet.
I am not the poetry.
Whatever I write is a contribution.
The poetry you hear is what I hear.

Table of Contents

Time	11
A Race or a Ride	12
Dear Bonnie	14
Venus and Mars	15
More Than a Minute	16
Navigation	17
Larceny	18
28 Lines	19
Blessings and Bruises	20
What Fish Don't Know	22
That's Why I Waited	23
Don't Forget	24
Calling Mr. Stevens	25
Luggages	26
Bizzy Bazz	27
Filters	28
Ask the Dealer	29
Crack Her Jacks	30
Practice Makes Perfect	31
Chin Hanger	32
Floccinaucinihilipilification	33
Dishabille	34
Feel My Wound	35
Certain Questions Answered	36
The Land of Prester John	37

Understand the Keen Toll	38
Harry's Touch	39
Lil Marleen	40
The Cork in the Bottle	41
All I Ever Wanted	42
A Suggestion for Peace of Mind	43
The Smut Inside	44
Population Growth	45
Death Looms	46
A Wrap and a Crap	47
The Monster Within	48
Result of Wedding	49
What Were You Thinking?	50
As the Church Dies	51
The Bridge	52
Late	53
Erato	54
The Secret of Aging	55
The Comma	56
Listen to Me	57
Imagicnation	58
OK, C'mon It's Talking	59
Bilious Commentary	61
I Grew Up in the Arms of Gods	62
Endgame	63

Global Heat	64
It's Not All Smirky Whoop	65
An English Garden	66
The World I Invented	67
This Night	68
As of This Moment	69
Influences	70
Am I a Cyborg?	71
The Art of Poetry	72
My Tippet Only Tulle	73
Up and Down the Aisle	74
Futility of Imagination	75
A Movement	76
The Editor Speaks	77
Musicals: The Old and the New	78
Under Siege	79
I Am a Mystery to Myself	80
The Cheering Section	81
The Radio is On	82
The Things of God	83
It's Coming	84
The Treatment	85
Angel Pens on Fire	86
Perfection	87
Training Plants	88

Beatataph	89
The Artist	90
The World Poet	91
The Edge of Extinction	92
Three White Leopards	93
The Dorian Invasions	94
Memory	96
Good to the Last Drop	97
Fig Tree	98
Tomorrow	99
Sæcula Sæculorum	100
Being Moved to Tears	101
Riffing with Rainer (The Convalescent)	102
Needle	103
Esperanza	104
Premeds	105
Antisthenes	106
Odious Comparisons	107
The New American Poet	108
Legacy	109
A White Elephant	110
Finally	111
The Momoment Arid Ved	112
Convenience Is Our Master	113
Eternity	114

Time

Here comes the poem called Time.
I am glad you came.
You like me and I like you.
Zucchini is your choice.
I like cucumber.
May no one ask why.

Am I out of the way yet?
Certainly I hope so.
Receptive is where I thrive.
But, o God, is it me?
No, it's not, it's the word
shaking the tree.

Emily, shut up.
You keep usurping
while I am burping.
It's so damn distracting.
You know I'm acting
on your behalf if anyone's.

The subject is this exploding moment
and you and whoever is paying
some purple attention
have invested what we have
what we laugh at
and the globe is blue.

A Race or a Ride

The hurdles before the ribbon are words
even if the ribbon is already split.
Always later than hoped for
beyond expectations the silly one eats.

It ain't me. It ate me. The sovereign power
leaves me in gray, the color of bemusement and shame.
Stop it. These moments could be precious
but are little more that what the grim process allows.

If we or me could freeze that swinging chair
from which all sitting is classical or holy,
but the instruments of engineering are obstructive
and, God knows why, the source of all grief.

The pink wants to interfere and mediate.
Pink's shroud is careless and jumps all over it.
The smile that I introduce and wait for the applause
is that same cloth I use to wipe the kitchen counter.

Always later than hoped for
some magic is supposed to be here.
The rabbits, the boxes, the smiling legs, the bustier
are irresponsible, because it's too serious for that.

In the back of the bus, something little creeps,
announcing that wherever this, what is this, leads
is to be taken lightly, if taken at all.
Where does that leave us? The next stop?

Even if the ribbon is already split
shadows and sun and fear of small spaces
will be our adventure, our crawl space,
our garden and our who knows what.

Dear Bonnie

You married a nutcase
who lives at night
waiting for the muse
and Canada whiskey
like canada geese
and xanadu cheese
to take effect and get
all right brain eddy
to fill sufficient space
and make the world
a better place.
It's the rhyme eddy
the co med dee
that always and also
shuts it up and down
and makes its mark.
The poet is a tattoo
upon the earth
which days are numbered
and his
in an unpublished book
hence unread and unreal
even if printed
but totally expected.
You know a this
and I know a that.

Venus and Mars

1
Changing places is not an option.
Horrified, too much, disturbed is better
by autobiography, whom did I love?
Mostly me I do think that's more honest
than I want to be. Great show
of whom I wish I was or could have been.
Falling all over myself, I remain
a fountain of obligations and the awful
absence of any right to decorations.
I'm reaching for something
that I cannot accomplish.
Something raw and completely responsible.
Not a chance. Too ingrained is
the excuse of mystery and whatever.
Let me know where they end up.

2
Squishing lovers at the opposite
ends of the love pole, the video
that promises collaboration,
and, moreover, punctuation dividing
the possible from the obvious
where most of us end up I'm sorry.
But what valiant souls that strive
for that blissful moment
only to discover time keeps
on ticking and what was that.
More choir than dance,
more zip than sh-boom,
more likely we're a couple
with him still wearing his stupid helmet
and her without a stitch on
waiting to slap him into a microwave oven.

More Than a Minute

It takes more than a minute
for that deep characteristic
to sink in enough to matter.
Commonplace is an artificial idea.
Here we go from where.

Let's for a moment dismiss,
ride out the pie charts and successive automobiles.
A little hunger space is placed between us.
Cram it with goodness and complicity,
a madame say or a quiet surprised virgin.

Eskimos, Samoans, Saroyans and plain sams
—all have some from some to some,
that interstice or fit of madness allowing
a pretty thing,
young touchless ambivalent potently yearning.
I want it to happen but so what…
With careful compromise you die no sooner.
I'm lying of course. All there is to do
—don't stop us—from that precious murmur
that spells itself…

Navigation

The sails are open;
Selections are upon us.
Please be candid if you are here at all.

There are so many wrecks on the road.
Will the constable please wait until we are through?
Again the directions are infamously wasted.

Our appetites are taking us by force.
O Madonna, the real one, talk please.
OK. I understand the satellite has difficulties.

You play with us—we poor and helpless.
If only I could manage to well
spring the project that God wants.

I don't know. By the way
that is the key you have all been
waiting for as if it were exciting.

Climb upon the shelves of books
that have told you already the
spot where you need not stop.

Larceny

Why must I always be the son
when I want to be sound or sane?
Then I find a dirigible in my casket
urging me on to the next circle.
The rainbow parked above me
speaks of obsession and aimless
cruelty to the minds of the turtles
that are part of the picture
whether we like it or not.
I can so go on like this.
Pieces of paper crumpled
on the blessed floor
—I am reminded of a sink
where ideas are tumbled
before drying on the roof.
It's cramped, it's crusty,
unnecessary, a bitty blasphemous
whenever I show up.

28 Lines

There is that crack in the ceiling which I love.
I love the crack; I love the ceiling.
It has been moving
all around the world I think.
I could eat it like an apple I love.
The apple does not eat.
Maybe it's my love that eats.

My question has to do with genes—
genes this, genes that.
I wouldn't care except I was misquoted.
Excuse me while I wait.
Sailing, sailing over the bounding main.
But home is a debt. We've been screwed.
Old Omar. His tent is all sewn up.

Don't say the center does not hold.
Big and swims with inflated wings.
Then comes out of the ducts and down the cheeks
the newly unified witness
to crimes and miracles.
When do I get to sleep?
Each day is covered by little cats' feet.

Not yet, not yet, cry the crows of mishap.
There is more danger to be found and to unfold,
cries the wiseass that creates my sometimes awful dreams.
You can't want it to be other-
wise; you can't really want it.
I have this smile that I beguile
and all the while I can't find the trumpet.

Blessings and Bruises

1   Language

Language is so frail.
It only begins to illume
the mysteries we save
to make disasters stop.

2   This Night Again

I will not let the fire be complacent.
Small energy it takes to poke it.
Flame is a witness to real burning.
Flame is drowsy and willing to quit.
Embers insist on meaning and voices.
Even as the glow grows shadows and so long.

3   The Idea of Making a Statement

Book spines, gold mines, paper skins,
as foul as fur, spray them with paint taint.
Give the thoughts back to the trees that made them.
It ain't the ratiocination or oration.
It's location, location, location.

4   Just a Name

Yes, I am louche
when I'm alone
only to cram
that last minute
with some foul
pleasant pleasure.
It makes my day.

5   Beefeater 24

Some people are weasels
hardly humane or human.
My breath is stolen.
I draw the shades.
The moonlight
drives me uncombobulate.
The security guard was
a prison guard and now
the world is upside down.

6   The Comb

When I found
her rattail comb
and let her have it
she took off
her mask
and hid that.

A few slaps later
out came the comb.
I slid off
into the dark
hoping the comb
would get lost
again.

What Fish Don't Know

This night won't stop,
I'm coming to the end of The Rock.

Don't argue about reality.
Try reality instead—modern values.

OK, let's do it again.
If a tree falls in the forest....

Of course, trees fall; of course, the forest,
the surge of words will delay us.

You have to be careful about where you park,
I choose, you choose, we all choose.

The blacksmith makes his life of iron.
Fish don't know that what they do is swimming.

That's Why I Waited

That's what I wanted
a little squeeze to make it pop,
a generous helping
so what would be at last
unnecessary and easy and give it up.

That urge to be beyond
so eloquent, so something or other,
that wants to get us off the dime
onto a spine, a life divine.
(No color just is, you know; we make it up.)

I welcome the transition
other English disappears and
Word—not Aramaic, not Greek, not Latin,
not Indo-European in any way.
Oops e daisy, don't need that.

Had I not been trained
what welcome may I have received.
I might have wandered,
pixilated into where belonging is,
shapeless, but spacious and pretty.

Priest will say what God is, or who,
but God has plenty to say, another oops,
when the time is ripe,
when you smoke your pipe,
when the time comes.

Don't Forget

A paleontologist is out there.
She recommends a chrome recipe
of where it all began.
You, silly, put your head in your hands,
spectaculating the implications that
she does not know what she portends,
and, of course, we all fall down.

Hypnosis might work
if you're extraordinarily fine china
or a toothbrush
worshipping a triangular bubbleprint,
leaving your hands free
to whittle something majestic
that will solve.

But don't forget blood, or
it will come back to haunt you.
How often have you heard
smearing the best joke
that you can never remember
until the spring uncoils?
Don't leave me alone like this.

Calling Mr. Stevens

Wallace stood in the middle of God
and wondered his life away.
I would be Wallace; I would wonder.
My eyes are catching up with this
—imagination that tears open,
reducing intelligence into peace.
A lioness recognizes me
allowing nothing but impulse
to focus her intentions.
I wonder to listen like that
—perceive and wait for it.

Luggages

A mindful of deviance;
Not solving the cryptic eternal puzzle;
Leaving so often;
Getting fired from the donut shop;
Not accomplishing the prime directive;
Knowing how to act but too late;
Being dumb;
All that I don't remember now;
The cats that went missing or died;
Not knowing when to stop;
Tinnitus;
Stealing books;
Of course, not knowing when to start.

Bizzy Bazz

The bizzy bazz for your razzamatazz
has melted in my pocket.
I am introduced as your relative;
mistakes are rampant.
Please excuse my whatchamacallit;
it's busy here in the library
and my foot is on fire.
Only to speak in couplets,
my heart is wasted and fool that I am,
can you lend me a couple of cups
before the roundness gathers?

Filters

Shit, my shoulder hurts!
It's not a circle on the ceiling,
although what fun that is.
A world full of targets more like it:
unscrupulous, marginal and learn-from-me.

Descending bars, ascending bars,
the work and time we put into it;
it being so thoroughly nebulous
as to be any adjective or adverb.
You can think what you want.

Why do I feel sorry now?
Did I kill a spark of invention
just to watch it die?
Or is it this room that annoys me?
Just to make it so?

Clam-more-rama approaching—
dial something nervous and exciting.
A positive response would have fire in it.
Don't tell me that I'm amazing, sell it.
I always wind up giving advice.

Ask the Dealer

Ask the dealer: ducks for bucks?
Do I want this ridiculous sense of peace?
Of course, from where else could it come?

My world has learned from paint
that eyes mean more than from conclusions
    wrought,
that sex requires restraint,
that anybody can be they who fought
to get their own brain straight.

A picture knows a truth.
It organizes words from here to death.
My eyes are true and mute.
I see my thoughts like they are changing breath.
A vision is the fruit.

Arena in Verona now.
A mine in Cornwall is forever gone.
One daughter loves her vow.
The sumac is New England. Fall is born,
it's only question how.

We're made to take a look
and so says paint this mind with mystery
as if it were a book
which God could with the help of me carry
and pix is all it took.

The painting reminds me of Cezanne.
Who the hell is Meyerowitz?
You want us to pay for it, don't you?

Crack Her Jacks

When you don't get it
is when you got it.
Seems simple but so are pajamas
or bananas.
Mother goosed you
and your smile is panoramic.
Over time Mother also molts.
Her lost feathers conspire
to make sense or
bend some off-the-track truth
still whistling in the dark.
The suspense is obvious.

Practice Makes Perfect

There are holes in the wall.
It is resembling Rome.
O, Good Lord, life and death,
I suppose, twisting in the wind…
Raw gourmet tasting for the lion
—not a pleasant thought, but
what would the movies do
without the specter and the zoom?
So few of us no matter how inept
get to be so lip smacking jolly,
do we, I'm asking, do we?

Such serendipities aside,
our silent demise is to be noted.
Write it down, damn it,
we came and we went.
Remember, though, there is
just one we.
There is just one cat.
There is just one species.
There is just one vast biology.
There really is just one vast,
and I'm proud and gratified
to be its member.

Chin Hanger

Back in the nest
identified as the forgiven
whatever falls in my beak
I follow and offer the guidelines
suspecting my indulgence
to be scrap metal at best.
Don't stop to think about it.
Just ingest.
OK in jest if you must.
Think about it.
Thank about it.
Forward and back
the little snack shack
where the muscles relax
and blinds are go-back.
That was the sneeze.
The bees' knees.
What do you want?
An exegesis?
A correspondence?
A tweet, God be said here.
One takes it back
there where the beak goes
at the back of the beak
to whatever follows the beak,
behind it, beyond it,
the amiable, unexpected,
constant, residing
sneeze.

Floccinaucinihilipilification

I get the floxy part
and I'm all about nihil,
but the pilification
leaves me cold and dry
like a bar drink
I just don't like.
If you're going to smart me
with cymbals and lyres
at least make it
a recognizable symptom
of a disease I know something about.

Dishabille

My spousal unit don't get
this poetry or funk.
Do I dispossess, divorce or worse?
No, there is always that chance
the bear will slumber in and
make the severest mimic of God.
Believe in her and believe me,
no matter how far we stray,
no matter the loss or grace
we get from the entire confabulation,
the world is not made of facts.
The world is made of our mistakes.

Feel My Wound

Have we slept on this street together?
Do we know each the concrete and the grime?
We don't want the pain
and we require as payment the end of it.
We have the pavement; we have the sleep.
An anchor trips the ship but not the sea.
The gutter is our beach; this stucco wall our palace.

If I'm looking down and dirty
and my knapsack isn't pretty,
look at the rainbow instead, you quirk,
there's always more to see than is apparent.
There's smelling pets and slugs and
emails my basic equipment don't get
because we live here half-hearted at least.

If we're going to talk danger
the suspects are abundant and grapeful.
My cracked nest egg is obviously safe
from whatever any devil has in mind
in the making of misery the best download ever.
I'm strolling away from this as if it never
let my pants decrease or my mother scold me.

Discover my meaning and plough it under
like I have small right to speak or wander
wherever the nose goes and the part in the hair
    disappears.
Tiny essences are blooming at the stop, and beasts
are stubborn in my cart. What improvement
is nascent and maybe happy to take my side?
When some dam makes a lake my heart breaks.

Certain Questions Answered

As the clock supposes, I am swimming in details.
Whom do I hate; what do I hate?
The measurement has yet to be invented.
Is Satan inside me? Do I reek?
Oh, they are bad. Those monkeys,
they make me squirm and think of
projection—the shadow that Jung,
that phlegmatic poseur,
makes me think of.
Now, when I most quiz it.
For God's sake, give me some room.
Does every thought have to be suspected?

May I not have flower arrangements?
Favorite songs? Indisputable color coordinations?
Why must it always be serious shit?
...that I stepped in despite warning my foot
to step elsewhere? Watch where you are
putting your foot down. Heavenly.

I got just as much right as anyone
to translate paradise into this—myself.
So there you have it, brothers and sisters,
the midnight we all were promised
is delivered.

The Land of Prester John

Looking for the perfect floor plan
coffee is missing; the sky
is introduced as Saturday.
Taking all the chance this moment
won't last forever unless who knows?

Danger is invisible
and the characters are few.
Is this the realm impossible?
Are those wires ceaseless?
Now our faux Eden next stop.

Attend the arteries and the dentist
No telling how long this heaving lasts.
Only I, no image, live inside me
"Here's some coffee." The big gets heard,
competing with tinnitus.

At the thin border of peace
stroll gratitude and enchantment.
Allow the family to sneak in.
Someone's slogging in the back rows.
It can't get better than this.

Then majesty arrives
as stupid as bees and as brave.
Don't say to me that some words
extend into these doppelganger universes.
Give it a short name and relax.

Understand the Keen Toll

I dial in 100.1 by the sheerest crevasse in audio engineering,
and what do I find? Some word flow by tengwar might help.
Don't take yourself too seriously it might say or the way
north is just as easy as west, east or south, without thinking
too much about it. The frown I see, the grayness of teeth
all tell me way too much about the thing I am pursuing
which God ordains must remain totally mysterious or why
do you bother, good friend, to keep waking me up in the
early morning before or after the sun comes home?

Harry's Touch

I have had "a little touch of Harry in the night."
"Where I am you may be also."
Think what you will I am intrepid to the end.
"Who would fardels bear?"
Think about that. And the perfect soul.
As kind and quiet and doing what needs to be done.
"Sir, I am not worthy to have you under my roof."
The world is made of brick and vines.
"Should! Should! Should! When will I ever learn!"
Ancient stuff is dark but thrilling.
And, o yeah, "the observer is the observed."
Commander, don't turn this ship around.
1 Corinthians 13 and "if by chance we get together
it's beautiful, and, if not, it can't be helped."
Sloping slips and Irene, good night.
"I say a little prayer for you."

Lil Marleen

I'm standing here
under the highlight
waiting for rain
beguiling my neighbor
and straining my name.
Herr this, Frau that,
yet stumbling yet
the room is smaller
and my what
grows paler.
It will happen here
while I'm standing
as sure as the dawn
is born stinking
a perfectly
useful dream.

The Cork in the Bottle

It's not about religion.
It's milder and sweeter even
than a cigar and grappa.
The place where I will be
is sunny and sandy
about a mile or so
from where I am today.
Casual geography
is my middle name.
Ignore girth
and wrinkles.
The transom over the door
is an escapade of escape.
Maybe that's religion.
One at a time take it.
Funny and bloated
a hidden drink
gathers in my toes.
I don't know religion.
I practice it.

All I Ever Wanted

Portensia is loose.
She might be making biscuits
which require no sense.
Importantly we bow.
I have probably crushed the wrong end,
favoring the tiniest of concepts,
the tertiary word or the last one.
Portensia speaks
as if she is dying and crazy with it.
She is not dressed for the occasion.
Why should she? Absence of paparazzi.
I keep listening as the band unfolds.
The definite rag, the mugging,
the kisses that hurt and signify.
Portensia, for God's sake, go to bed.
We may have a quiz tomorrow.

A Suggestion for Peace of Mind

Let them see me in an open casket with a waxen face.
An eternal moment is their privilege as it's mine.
My face, my moment, their moment and their face.
Such should be (God, did I say should?) any moment.

Open wide your heart, your face, your eyes, your life.
Make it, take it as it is, knowing as it was.
The ship's away, another day, we always say
there I go as he goes, we all go. Like a day.

Slumber is an introduction to eternal space,
the place where mountains grow and seas subsume.
You don't need a resume to get there.
Leave your coat at the check-it-here place.

The Smut Inside

Thinking about you every day.
White smoke from the exhaust
I'm told is bad sign
that the engine needs to be encouraged
or remounted or scratched.
Attention need not be paid.
I ride the bad smoke
until the rain scotches it
and the dry path I wander
comes back of course to haunt me.
I love the way you taunt me
but you have no idea.
I have a shelf of days that I sort
and you are a delta of sin.
I don't admire me.
I have a delta of mud and New Orleans
—that weather that stinks and kills.
May I leave the room for a minute?
Anger and lost moments are now suppressed.
I am an animal.
God bless us everyone.

Population Growth

We are the billions now on this planet.
Derangement is to be expected and
less than that speaks is not honest.
It ain't who's the hottest
It ain't who's the smartest.
Most of us are bilious or smarmy and
if you let us we are self-congratulatory.
What else do we expect?
We are the mushrooms
and charity is our challenge.
But don't forget that we will die.
Ain't that John Donne
or Christ even better?
Or Buddha for that matter?
Or Allah or whoever matters
for that matter,
Cuz matter, matter, matter.

Death Looms

Ok, I read it.
Actually, I read it twice.
Redact it, say you. Red act?
Where does responsibility begin and/or end?
The bees have it.
So do hummingbirds.
Six inches more or less from your nose,
They incredulously fly.
Think of it—fly!

Insomniacs live here.
We always can catch up though
maybe a day or two after.
If we knew we had those days…
They are expensive.
Do you have a better word?
Do you know words better?
Have you been to Seattle or Oregon?
Then but not only then talk to me.

The hummingbird was Anna's,
—the only species in this state,
colorlessly drab and wonderful she was,
or he if she were immature.
I've lost the train.
Fear not, ambulances are available.
I'm waiting at the moment.

A Wrap and Crap

If I were complacent
and did no work or corruption
could he who
makes a difference not know
I am adjacent.
Jack Sprat
who splintered and disposed
of himself and elevators
sees me and who knows
what or who he really loves.
Of course bassackwards
is a method and a dose
of the smelliest, forgivingest
particle of a word
that intrudes exposing
the louse I am and
the louse I am meant to be.
Analysis is a proclivity
that you were meant to see
and missed it
by a mile may I say.
You left me here
a total stranger
and I mean total
to foray and spray
not responsibly
but invention is the game.
So personal,
so in your face.

The Monster Within

Try trading places with a sleeper.
He or she will shame you
with his or her concomitance.
To you, my friend.
To me, as well.
We are the giants.
We are the elves.
We are superimposed on the map
that leads us to
whatever smells like
or feels like
that next thing
that greets us,
that obeys and smites us.
It's that sense of belonging
that betrays us
and squeals on us
saying whoever we truly are.

Result of Wedding

The first I married was…
The second was aspic.
The third was Tom Mix,
or was that the night
my ears waxed a fabulous number?
Always the joint I'm dreaming.
Hiding, sliding, abiding,

never the true awful text,
but always the glamorous number.
It's not just a gratifying spell;
it's a stumping, cryptographic,
rubbery, pulse jamming number.
Uncomfortable as well
and escapingly specific.

Wrap whatever is my mind
around the hers of old moments
and include the joint? The third!
I died, will die, with that
our love is not a number,
cuz the puddle moves
not only the canoe but the water.

What Were You Thinking?

Seed follows gigantic implausible idea
then grows then grows without profit or reason.
God steps in and speaks (implausible and what
 profit?)
his name: (unspeakable but what the hell…) I yam.
Thanks. Where now? What now?
The serpent wants you to know.
The serpent is messing with your dreams.
If you love your life,
be grateful.
Grapes, dreams, stew
—have a smile day.

As the Church Dies

The facilities are cramped.
Allegiance is in dispute.
The mangos, oranges and persimmons
all scream bloody betrayal.
Saints are here to help us
understand, they say; I say
what were you thinking?
We were made to wander.
No wonder all we do is wonder.
We are wonderful, look!
When two or three…
But who's counting?
To understand we were not meant.
We are thrown out of the temple.
Show me the money.

The Bridge

So many ways to be misunderstood
and so little to understand
 —maybe Eurydice said to care about
the misunder and the under.
When I'm at the wheel and the road
looks for me to like it,
the shortest distance is
invariably the longest.
Just like the weed set in
over the 1959 bridge
which was two ways on one level
and on the level at least two ways.
I don't know how long this is going to take.

Late

An amber light sneaks over a photo frame
where Fred, our cat, is seen, ears up, paws out, sunning
on a square of ultraviolet light which deepens the dark
shadows needing Photoshop (registered trademark
by Adobe) fixing. What happened just now?
Just the pen and the page sneaking up on the hand,
the wrist, the arm, the shoulder, the neck, the…

Erato

So glad to have met you at last.
Yes, I cheated on you,
but only before we were married.
We married and then met.
You gave your word; I gave you mine.
Sure, I forgot it now and then.
Do you remember what I said?
We scraped against each other
on a street where the lamps blinked.
You had a flashlight;
I had a candle.
Do the blind see light?
Why are you yelling at me?

The Secret of Aging

And this is where legends cry.
Rockets and shuttles keep them dry.
How many bulbs to screw in takes
our hands, our minds and then our stakes?
A dropdown menu cools our heels.
Electricity flies our wheels.
Our ears are padded without fears.
This will go on for many years
until starvation makes us bold.
It's overrated to be old.

The Comma

Hercules had a tumor
that kept him indoors.
His strength was a legend,
but he had mini force.

The disease that betrays us
is only admired
by the stump that thought Jesus
would disappear soon.

Yet the phrases he spoke
haunt us when we sigh.
He could have said it.
Did you hear it? Did I?

Earth has one moon.
There is only one cat.
Am I smiling?
Or did I just fat?

Listen to Me

I use a common tender to buy
not resorts, not cuisine, not
the approval of saints.
My tender has its own
pretentious useless go away.

The numbers of it sway piddling
always looking for the universes
said to be so much banging.
No such as a straight line.
It's a wiggle and a wonk and a wiper.

Up now and attending the fog
calling itself with notes of truffle,
not pleasing you, not again
any animal whose right brain
has a price tag or a resourceful countenance.

We know what not is. What is is
comes out like nasty shellfish or
miseries that words don't match.
O God, give me a home where the buffalo.
O God, listen to me not away the day.

Imagicnation

In the crosshairs
Pumping pious prigots preen
Return to sender

The steps are cold
Wetdays come and gone
Open a mask

Sensible fare
More bodies to see
Crenelate the border

A floral floor
Mixtures of friendship
The boat is full

OK, C'mon It's Talking

Dig yourself a hole.
Follow the instructions on the box.
Please God my fingers are weary.
What does it cost here to dance?
Olé! I dropped the nickel I shined
to get as far as this. Ambiguous.

Am I lazy or stupid?
Serenely they bite their collective tongue.
I mean one... I see him... Pop him.
I will never outpedal this drift.
Rimbaud be damned. A fraud
if I've ever seen one...
If I've ever been one...
The screen is fuzzy but not blank.

Several hundred years have past
since we last heard from you.
We are absurdly excited about what's next.
I have translated the static.
—fitfully, and off the page to be sure.
Are you saying nonetheless the flowers or something?
Yeah, I love the old stuff but not now.
To face this painting of myself
lost in a thought that is forbidden and
all kinds of quasi and pseudo and fun key...

In the name.
OK, C'mon it's talking.
Of the father.
We're used to saying flesh and blood.
Let's just say instead whatever it is you did.
And of the son.
Extreme magic and numerous puzzle speak.
Absolute imperative sine qua non instruction.
The love bug.
And of the holy spirit.
Humans think reality.
Reality thinks itself.
What's beyond obvious?
Look who's talking now.

Amen.

Bilious Commentary

This is when the voices arrive.
Time is said which should not be said.
After all, I have to deal with urination.

God help you and your flowers.
Speak to me only in your guise.
I come with a sword so take it from me.

Should I resemble the impossible?
What could it mean? Major Sensible
says take your seat. I will measure

any table for which you feel
responsible with a mangled edge
and the juice you came here with.

I am not gullible.
I am not supercilious.
I am just who you think I am. Amend.

I Grew Up in the Arms of Gods

Thank you, Friedrich, I copy that.
Biceps, triceps, extensors and flexors.
There had to be a rescue.
But Gods? Are you kidding me?
My molecules betray me.
Or whatever level of sophisticated
anatomical and biological
and micro and meta biological…
Got lost. Sorry. Meant to stay intact.
I want the arm of God.
Squirrel down and lift me
away from the finite or infinite.
Let this moment
be, oh I don't know, creative
or sex with my mother, forever.

Endgame

Mercy will follow us
wherever shall she lead.
The minute she abandons us
our faults in us she sees.
I cannot feel the fault in us.
What would the mailman say?
Our breath is not so fabulous
to make us to obey.
I dreamed last night
an omnibus that took me to Land's End.
It was all right
but not for it to send
me on my way to God knows where
some pub or skittle fare
where "Will you take me in?"
was "What are you—more than air?"
an imagined secret, a dream
(I say so I don't get arrested)
that didn't actually happen
but what's the harm in thinking
it might have. Mothers
are ageless targets of our rage.

Global Heat

By cracky, the indispensible is spent.
It's dark in there—busted axons, gilded neurons,
kinesins tied up in traffic, living without names.
The magic of brain metered down to feet—chronic.

The establishment is out of its own control.
Birds are shrinking and they call off key.
The way out is the way in and it's through.
It's funny peculiar; not funny hah hah.

All the admixtures come out odd.
Just so many hops and go to jail.
That stupid space between our toes
resembles more and more our mania.

Small comfort to be dead.
Most animals don't live long either.
Why am I listening to this stuff?
Item: holding on the swinging pearly gates...

It's Not All Smirky Whoop

A dark smoke line crosses the page.
Snake eyes or God's eye crosses the page.
I tremble at the feet.
Give me garlic, garnish, grammar or grass,
but not this harmony that my feet
don't understand, don't stand over,
don't toe the line, or don't scan.
Whither now goes my earnest mind?
All foot and finger and dangle go I,
back to the immoderate—the unascending.
Black spots, inkish, inkling, inky
splurts that stop and giggle
at temporary anguish wandering…
So high, I can't get over it;
So low, no way under it.
It's not all smirky whoop.

An English Garden

Those are *insights*, spectacular, but sparse.
Over here we have *regrets*. They don't
bloom long; they're small and very white.
Don't step on the *memories*, so fragile,
hard to see, long stems, but tiny petals.
The bugs love the ordinary *thoughts*
while the slugs love these fine *moments*.

My mother made pies from the redolent *charity*
and fertilized the *indictments* with reeking compost.
My father preferred annuals like purple *jokes*
and was especially fond of the yellow *curses*.
Myself I prefer the fragrant *prayers*
and dismiss the ground covers
such as this trampled *thyme*.

The World I Invented

Not me, it's Orpheus, so unassuming
makes us abashed and barely caring,
It was he who took the route that
silly and ghoulish has us grinning.

Not yet, maybe, but when we get it
our noses will greet our eyebrows
and our ankles be blessed with horns
and our wrists with comely trinkets.

Not now, because the words alarm us
and send us seeking for comfort
as if that was the modus operandi
that will give us orgasms and hope.

Not while the ships and airplanes,
the nuclear whatevers prosper,
until we are ghosts scheming
to make the world, yes, invented.

This Night

This night being not the last
is also the note begot
and hidden from my real life.
Tales of South Africa
soon to be forgotten
were born this afternoon
and eve. And Eve visited
Adam again. Will he ever notice?
I don't want to be Adam
again but am I not helpless?
I shiver in the heat
and sweat in the Arctic.
That's not who I really want to be.
I want to be South Africa,
a Boer and a boar and borrower
if I could only shape up.
Mom, you are intrepid
to have lasted this long
telling me to keep trying.
Mom, you are a tale
of South Africa
and the spirit still
of Mary Baker Eddy.

As of This Moment

I'm here with this brain
a midnight and later refrain.
It's a compass I confess
and detest as it respires.

Any moment jewels will come
and I most likely will be numb.
The consequence I do not fear
will be it instigates my ear.

All of which I resonate
as if it complicates my fate.
But God knows nothing
unless it rains and that's his game.

Plow the earth if you must.
Nothing but dust and more dust
is the legitimate outcome.
The rest is in the ocean.

Influences

> *Life's nonsense pierces us with strange relation.*
> —Wallace Stevens

Possibly an illness I could not name.
Dagger in the back. Collars round the throat.
Here and there a line that led astray.
Geometry, possibly.

An idea of order with concordant voices
and then the rat smell and oranges galore
start in the back and move up.
Natural is a big, ugly, happy word.

We can all expect a variety of strokes
which may enable or disable our desire to make good.
Take away the clubs and spades—black by chance.
Leave the diamonds and the hearts—red instead.

Where did all this come from? Fact is I didn't.
Something in the sky refrains my brain and burns it,
brands it, demands it, scans it and prepares it.
I am never alone when I'm by myself.

Am I a Cyborg?

At an edge where titanium and stainless steel
hold the balance when a streetlight fails.
Believing is seeing. Who cares is a beach,
invitation to absurd numbers and crackpots.
Blind alley sufficiently open to speculation
is breathing the way monuments take air.
Just suppose a three-legged animal
sharing your razor, your cologne, your hopes.
You're still at home with those various whatever
that silence you, make you daft, feel like cotton.

Another sip means another sort of contention:
that eating, etc., are patterns of almighty creation,
downbeats, so thorough, so anonymous, so many meows.
Surrender is a viable preoccupation that answers
whoever is asking. Let's pretend a smile will stop it.
You think an image will maintain your whereabouts?
But biology damns us and keeps us awake.
There for the sake of someone or what go I.
It's in the right brain the real dots are suspended,
just a piece of mind, a thing, the actual peace.

The Art of Poetry

Each page sports a smudge.
The interference of parents
random as houses
packing hunches as lunches
say eat me, it's about us.
Like puppies, I suck it up.
The good old me we
— that's the beans I am.
I suck in my speak
even hearing the link I crave.
I'm ringing the connection.
Pick up! Wake up! Talk!
Trite dead silence is my curse.
Now, of course, the mentor won't
give the time of smelly day.
His height is not amused.

My Tippet Only Tulle

I don't know what real is.
Something bumps into something
I suppose. I suppose, you say,
God knows so we don't.
Sure I eat granola;
I sing about Cape Cod;
I try to condole those
who grieve, who are elastic.
Still I have cold shoulders.

Up and Down the Aisle

God, you make me write
like a whipsaw in the freezer.
This child is mine, I say,
the tumblers, the latch, the bolt lock,
all mine; I can hardly twist
or kneel, or bow, or shake,
because this little Jesus is mine.

I go to church on my little legs,
with my small mind on crutches.
There's food from the heavens they say
and my tiny stomach
in fractious with faith
that walking and eating are possible,
that our maids are all in a row.

The angels cry, of course,
why else could they matter?
Bumpy pews without seat belts,
nonetheless I am astonished
being assaulted by the liturgical plan
that grows like moss in the damp,
impenetrably sweet and often dour.
Nonetheless, the less is none and amen.

The aisle is swept by the crucifer.
The celebrant rains on our spectacles.
The floor reaches up to be holy.
God, when do I stop?
The child is all over me.
My hair has gone far and out of reach.
The recession is complete.

The Futility of Imagination

Finally and for a moment a steady hand.
John Coltrane, need I say more?
The ash is only as good as the fire was.
But ash is ash even as the fire gropes.

Sharing blankets across all years,
ears making covenants that swell,
the romance of language and bread
—what do you see? What do I?

I can't make tails or heads. Not my job.
Spit a pic and wipe your chin.
Rejectamenta is sarcastic and applicable.
Scorn not the corn that wears the crown.

A smile hides in a title and always has.
At some speeds the neck breaks and
tawdry morning closes to spirit afternoon.
The space between apple and sad makes if funner.

A Movement

Can I have the honor this hour
of dancing with you?
There is a curse in my pants
and a crease.

Give me a chance.
Let's explore the oval
as well as the resonator.
Somewhere in there
is a space (it's a spark)
is something to be seen.

My daddy had bones,
a sense of rhythm.
He came and went.

To be honest as Egon,
had I been him
I would be dead
these last thirty-eight years.

...that much
for painting beyond the possible,
like Ivo on the piano.

The Editor Speaks

Panama, Raisinhead, Crumbucket is losing his balance
in order, order is the word, to gain stasis, something
more intelligent, having sacrificed that for stupid, and coming
back again with the other brain side, knowing now
right from left, the stroke, the connection, the crossword
that intercepts the antecedent, the precedent and the now, so
stupid is the way to grow and thinking is a habit.

Musicals: The Old and the New

My son, my son,
so many figures to deduce,
so many steps, so many moods.
In the aorta, in the brain
the management leaves it open.

If it were spanish moss
it would subside in the shadows
comely and perturbed,
a rhythm scratched and uttered,
so take it out.

There is no earthly use
neither damage nor corrigible inspiration;
home always happens where the heart.
I'm slamming the door
but heaven is still open.

Go, son, go.
The management is stupid
and wants to be ordained
because the reason is pellucid
and somewhat shifted in a strange way.

Under Siege

Glamour is just too fussy for this night;
let's benign instead.
There's room for smelling salts.
I forget their assigned destination.
I'm just crap at making dings right.

All I want is to make it right.
You can say compass. You can say dreams.
But I don't remember the Alamo.
Take me away from the short end.
I style myself as the long guy with long shorts.

What rendition is better spoken?
Passers-by that lose their way?
Incremental dangers requiring to be ignored?
Stupid questions?
Arbitrary memories that have their faults?

Claim me. Stain me. Be a brave me.
Unstuck, this little pig will not harm nor swallow.
Wallow, little pig, until tomorrow.
That's only if you show up at the bus stop,
especially with everyone wandering around as they do.

More yet, always more yet.
O I am listening tonight.
One of those moony pizza in your eye nights,
not too fussy, just right. Pass the salt.
I just escaped from the Alamo.

I Am a Mystery to Myself

The batter is in a slump.
In the box, cleated, tarred,
what's called a pitch
sooner than not
inevitably delivered
(excitement, concern,
determination ensues)
all in a twitch,
waiting impossible,
for God's sake, swing!

The Cheering Section

This premature act of observation
is you got sense use it.
If realms of quizzes haunt
the spaces between your teeth;
if you got them, just heed.
I dumbellishly value all
that hides in gutters and on towers.
They are destinations not taxis.
To find is to seek and verse is vice.
Well, maybe color plays
whatever you roll in but
for your eyes only and
what a blessing to see.
What else you got?
Let me hear you say it.

The Radio Is On

Just a little dust.
Just a little ash.
Suspended particles cute
when we are children;
then in your face when
you're old, piecemeal,
and bloodshot and waiting.
Come back, little rocket;
it's early enough.
The sun is ashinin'
and love is so tough.
Amazing, ain't it?
That mother waits,
and father waits
and all their mothers
and all their fathers
wait, wading in clouds,
suspending and suspecting
our furious arrival,
as if they didn't get it.

The Things of God

In the beginning was the title.
That's all it was. X is given.
Make of it what you will
And your will disappears in heaven.
Chase the cheese, of course, but
give up your remorse.
Someone will absorb it
for no apparent reason.
Your reward may be pain or peace.
You make pain of the peace
or peace of the pain.
Whatever, you are always welcome.
Sure it's a stretch and I'm a wretch,
a wretch within reach and forgiven,
given even before I'm forgiven.
That's the word.

It's Coming

Another crash test is coming.
So many people. So much to lose.
Blood, booze, bitterness and blackmail fail.
Master the moment we are told
just as the door slams.
Who's talking now?
Strength being just the other side of weakness
and nothing is adequately explained.
Where are the knights? Where the splendids?
Accuracy does not interfere or intercede.
Why do you think I am on my knees?
It's a pisser. It's bad. I am forlorn.
The aisle is long; the walk is slow,
but over before you know it.
Sweet confusion, the princess might assist
but she trips on her train.

The Treatment

Give up the personal in this, old boys.
There just might be something for some
that bings and bangs, sidesaddlely corrupting,
that finds the river smooth and justified.

She threw me a kiss; that's not so much.
Moments matter like it or not or love theme.
I yield, you yield, we all yield.
Numbered days make daisies wave.

I wear penetrable armor like moving sand.
The harps I hear have a hippie hoppie leak.
There is no other place to go but here.
So, don't take me back; just kiss me.

Beyond is welcome; the party is catered.
We did not have the time but we could pay.
You are welcome. Our sleazy ways are ours.
Your patience is accepted; so laugh now.

The cross-eyed bear speaks up and at me:
Do I understand what life dreams?
Might mean no asking, just kneel and gesture,
and the smoke and song will catch you.

Angel Pens on Fire

Are you comatose? Your face.
Let the blue lights up and at 'em.
Rings receive what squares reject
while the burning is restrained.
Commander, tell us when to let loose
our fusillade, our flame, our burst
of carnivorous cantankerous blams
to let others know they are in our light
and to step aside and believe
we can be no more outrageous
than light, odor, body, edibility or spite.

Perfection

Jesus popped in from the Near Orient.
I entered from Providence Plantations
where confusion and conflict reigned.
Jesus reigned over tricks and anger
with a team of Christians that vie
to keep going in one direction and flail.
No stranger to conflicts is Jesus.
Poor God, trying to orient us
to get that perfection is lovely and horrific.
Our perfect we are sure is more
perfect than God's. So blaming God
is also perfect I imagine. Welcome
to the perfection that is what it is,
ipse ergo it doesn't get any better
than this and you've got to love it
or be miserable. Have mercy.
Take it from the lamb and be good.

Training Plants

My molecules can't expand
to satisfy the feeling
that certainly must resemble love.
She deserves a sun-soaked island
to grow everlasting plants
whose flowers do not satisfy
themselves.
She wouldn't call it tragic.
She would rebel against
their limitations
and make them speak a language
she and only she would understand.
She should have better flowers.

Beatataph

A scoundrel has appeared
in the headlights.
Many species are drifting
irresponsibly asunder.
What to make of this?

When I'm dead and gone
a prophet will wake up
and mend a million others.
Boy, do they have their work
cut out for them.

I will be so sleeping
as not to notice
what I was alive
and where was I before.
It's the chance we take.

Speaking of chances,
have you seen the dice?
The dots are melted.
The sides are ice.
Make nothing of it.

I'll be back for breakfast.
Smile at me then
when I'm most believing
when the sin of dreams is gone
and I'm ready to fling.

The Artist

Am I a genius yet?
Am I Vincent?
Am I Emily?
Our toes were similar.
Is that not enough?
Is not my speculation
and my skyrill
up to the mark
of ochre and green
spread without thought
of generations
of fine art
and crooked syntax
and the glorious
ultimate tax
we can't afford
by the way
and taste?
Taste?
Be serious.
Is it me?
Or the drink?
Or the chutzpah?
Or the magnificence
of not knowing how
differences are made,
or of how the world
is made of styrofoam?

The World Poet

He grieves so hard outside the now
—all then-forth and then-back.
Maybe even indifferent to when
—just mad about it. By mad I mean
just fucking furious.
He makes everything disappear
except the nouns of fear,
the verbs of horror,
the pronouns of the dead,
and the adverbs of anguish.
His eyes and ears are memories
and dire expectations.
Of course, he probably has it right.

The Edge of Extinction

The relation of incidents corrupts our brunch
making us believe it will never stop.
Does not each span of a homo sapiens
conceive the universal waft of explosions?
Did not the maid clean up the junk
that meanders through another day and dollar?
Look at the squiggle in the lower right corner.
That's the signature of the imperturbable.
Asking directions is futile exercise
—being lost in the moment is the most acceptable.
Convince me that biota, flora and rocks
are the final trick and the end of chance.
I will call your sanguine full house
knowing that this flush is always ready.

Three White Leopards

If any thought was meat
like days ground down
to the end of thought.
Lady, we are flesh et cetera.
Make less of it
than it appears to be
—and apothegm to be forgotten
like a hungry beast
licking its chops—any beast.
Remembering and forgetting
are so much alike,
as much alike as caring
and not caring,
having been cared for
most substantially.

The fault, Lady, is under our feet.
Stretch down your toes.
You think it's sand but
it has no odor, no measure,
no consequence or prize.
It's just your feet and something.
The stretch is good
and some kind of discovery
is like being alive,
worth your while.
It's good to love
and it's good to die,
worth your while.

The Dorian Invasions

1
"The meaning of the concept has become to some degree
    amorphous. "
Well, of course, all degrees and concepts and becomings are.
What makes me think of centipedes and millipedes?
Are they not the universe and every thought
that the bathers have as they undertake purity
and the responsibility of being the caretakers of any old
    rings?

2
"The work done on it has mainly served to rule out
    various speculations. "
Working on the shadows that come tonight in spite of our
    egregious behavior,
having spoken frankly and absurdly to all who are
    involved in this
faulty and hopeful spectacle that goes well with gin and
    tonic,
and with the hopes and fears of all our years, nameless
    and strong.
I can only cram so much into the wicked cerebellum that
    grins despite.

3
"The possibility of a real Dorian invasion remains open."
O Lord, tell me aubergine and zucchini and the wishes of madness
are not also terrible and welcome signs that help us with nutrition.
It seems so obvious that I'm open to any aphorism that speaks.
I'm passing on the frugal, blended, skinless cracks that maybe sustain
but don't they also pain us so that our backsides are smitten?

4
Resplendent in their tutus and wings come the divers to ask us.
Why do you keep reminding us of our spurious condition?
Don't we have enough to deal with without you constant intermission?
Give us back what we lost. Give us the frown of recognition.
Give us the house that won't break. Give us the ambition we need
to make the land stop heaving and the sky to wail unconsoled.

Memory

Let's look at the master bedroom.
The Gloria the Agnus Dei the Credo
are abiding in there peacefully
for the moment at least but
what else you got.
A walk-in closet and nothing to hide
not even leather breaches
or a false cock sling
or any other appurtenance
that would make a normal person blush.
We've kept it clean so far
and with as much as anyone knows
whatever is revealed
is of minute unencumbered interest.
The en suite however is frank
and hard to miss.
The prevalence of water
in our bodies
and in our amenities
is so awfully obvious
inescapable and delirious
it makes it hard to care about.

Good to the Last Drop

I don't argue with whatever
people think time is.
Whatever is come and gone,
not even a mouse.
If there is a distance
it's miles well spent.
A carafe, some bread,
a fancy feeling with
undisclosed limits,
all inside unsure of where
outside is playing.
I think it is a mistake to think
my brain is where it ends.

Fig Tree

Danger is always imminent.
Even manure and hoeing may not save us.
If we don't produce
comes the hack, hack, hack.
Well, produce, or something like it.
Hunger abounds and more than
lack of laziness is not enough.
Bring that, cook it, pass it on.
Whatever you've got.

Tomorrow

> *I am moved by fancies that are curled*
> *Around these images, and cling:*
> *The motion of some infinitely gentle*
> *Infinitely suffering thing.*
> — T. S. Eliot

Climbing over caustic inertia,
developing spots on my skin,
I see the ocean as peculiar
as if it were dim or dumb.

The clams are gone; so are the bones,
Nothing here but sand to use
for counting the suns of the universe
as if verse were merged one.

Snot. Never was. Can't be.
My wicked methods won't allow it.
Who is saying this?
Does she wear garters and pearls?

Trouble with listening comes
aloof and hardly articulate.
Bicycle spokes and ears of corn.
Serenity is not part of it.

The class is restless and the teacher smirks.
We're reaching down an alley for a melody.
She makes my fingers shake and shape
a meticulous adventure in a jungle of swans.

The name of the place is going home.
My sad, poor, lousy ocean
cannot compete with all the acts
and facts that organize the next day.

Sæcula Sæculorum

One cannot focus
on the putrid passing
of colorless night.
When you turn off the light
right brain hears the mayhem.
Chiarascuro patrols
and conquers the dark.
It is a responsibility.
Not what we should
but what we could do.
Be it an angel,
a sprite,
an equation,
or tavern songs,
emotional crises,
an indoor plant,
a series of lies,
more bloody destiny
than we can think of,
the music of horses,
the roar of an old Saab,
the failure of a toilet,
the chance of a good meal,
what arrives between our legs
by happy chance
   —this congregation of what happens next
I think is what I'm allowed to pray with.
I am still naked;
I am not quiet;
I'm water and air
almost congealing
to some blistering evermore.

Being Moved to Tears

> — *about Brahms' Opus 118, No. 2*

What are you ripping?
You snuck in and made a garden in my ears.
Oh yes, sonorous and empathetic and o look a surprise,
but why why why do you insult me like a buzzing fly?
Then you lie down like a hip, a thigh, the crisis
behind a knee, not to mention that stupid wet stream
that now adorns and adores my stupid cheek,
not my bottom cheek but my thinking cheek,
the cheek on my face that I prize of my mind,
that doesn't really know what cheek it prefers.
I apologize for the ignorance of my distraction.
Damn, the piano is an ungrateful animal
that throws our minds, hearts, whatever
like we don't appreciate what we are,
and then because of you, Johannes,
you the middle meddler of music,
we are faced with our wet faces.

Riffing with Rainer (The Convalescent)

This noise called a what? A song.
I hear it because my ears are smug.
Precisely precious and crookedly crowed
--this song belongs to a troubled street.

Her voice is not measured or free.
Notes bend beyond gauge or chance.
The grass reminds her of growing, so
what slips and creaks is blended.

I don't love the crown she wears.
A mistake is to make too much of her.
She sufficiently touches her sufficient self.
She doesn't crave what she wants. She sings.
It's my ears that save her, aimlessly.

Needle

Orpheus, come home. The sheets are clean.
Where are you when you're not here?
Said the jealous jongleur I'm sure.

Visit, he cries, as if distressed,
as if undressed and not so shy about it.
Such is the path that bucket carriers trod.

I am a friend I insist, a proper ditty box
to put the buttons on the mystery.
God only knows the garment that needs it.

Esperanza

Is it too late? A brain blanket? A supreme fiction?
The prize we keep our eyes on? Incomprehensible?
These shifty eyes immersed in a spectrum of possibilities
have come a long way in which long has no meaning.
Shake it and the fruit falls at our foot.
Mama made the sun rise and the moon to boot.
Twinkle the map and the road shines.
The direction, the fog, the miasma, the spirit
—what do they orate? The means of thinking
gives us all the room we need to make it up.

Petmeds

It's like I have fleas, so please
it isn't space that I need
but greedy me that's what I'll take.
My baby brain just don't get
that science knows me or cares.
I need the care and God is there;
God, who loves science and loves me,
is there, accomplish, effervescent,
sensible, sizeable and with no measure.
Anybody can say God and
not know what they mean.
Count me among them.
Count me.

Antisthenes

This is the twenty-first century.
Every room has been rented.
Nothing is grown that is not eaten.
Crowds glow and believers scream
an ultimate transmorgified misery.

I am relieved to say goodbye.
My Toyota is having a fit and cries
the way a twitter leaps into disguise.
Give me back my pancakes and boiled eggs.
I need a moment or two before expiration.

The secrets and tricks of dying
as a method of making me feel better
are lost in the clutter of those few thoughts,
the meander in Athena's garden and her height.
Sorry to be so cynical but fuck it.

Odious Comparisons

> Things won are done; joy's soul lies in the doing.
> — Shakespeare, *Troilus and Cressida*

Microchannels within the cerebellum
do not resemble bricks or mortar.
There is more confabulation
in heaven and earth
than the scowls of merchants and priests
are aware of or even care about.

Emotion is practice.
There are odds in thoughts.
The cream of the crop
disappears in the macrobottom.
Areolas are active contributions
to the mass of grinding it out.

So I think what I want to think.
Words are not as handy as expected.
The dimensions of idea
have no respect for space.
I surrender my obsession
as the petal to the stem.

The New American Poet

Don't ask me to say what a poem means.
Don't ask me if I understand my dreams.
I don't; I can't. There is no love in that.
Philosophers are trained to spread the crap
that our existence is to be explained.
Cause is a slave and the effect inane.
And the inspiration always comes to tears.
A poet is the ape of years and ears.
And in my case the truth is simply crass:
that Robin Blaser fucked me in the ass.

Legacy

Don't read it. I don't care.
Go jump in the reservoir where
microscopic entities are at war.
When you get to the truth of that
proceed to relieve in the big water
with your yellow sensational cocktail.
A molecule in the ocean can be found
wherever the other molecules have gone.
No disaster, just fate, and possibly heaven.
Let's all go find the ocean.

A White Elephant

Und dann und wann ein weißer Elefant.
    — Rainer Maria Rilke, *Das Karussell*

Rick Duerden gave me a bronze animal,
tusks, severe hide, insistent stance, spacious
and comfortable as was the world we lived in,
sans taste, sans agreement, sans rejection,
a globe without any sense except song.

How could I not jump on it,
thinking also of dogs, wives,
the ocean and wood? One remedy
was present; what we longed for lived
—a castle without rent or crazy concern.

There are such times that are divine,
when age flows back like stupid water
and the skills we're told to gather
are as useless as alarms and shaving.
We made our cots and slept in them.

Finally

I am going to make tomorrow as small as possible
in case some squad with merits and sinews comes along
to prevent the final explication of the truth as we know it
to be, flexible but incontrovertible and awkward,
as we all are not mentioning any immediate family.

I take all the responsibility for any misunderstanding
leading, of course, to the inevitable "No I don't want dessert,
I will be happy with an espresso and a little care."
Fat chance, my friend, I say give us more room,
more space to be our ridiculous selves, discerning.

There is what to eat and what not to drink
that will allow us to assemble in the hall
without mistakes, without our incredible baggage
which should have been checked in at birth
before we knew what we were in for.

It's creepy, insoluble, not what we wanted
but say it again the problems are beyond us
and hope says leave us alone to muddle
as we do around the last moments allowed us
at this terrible moment of reckoning.

The Momoment Arid Ved

Have you been listening?
Our cemetery is open now.
It's sticker time
but after Thursday it's gone.
You takes your chances
and if it don't work
so many memories
that don't amount to much
are your silly legacy.
What were you thinking?
Big black irises
dancing across the vroom
have as much sense
as any of us make the
turbulence that accommodates
our empty graves
our measures of time
our splot back space
where the neighbor
we truly love
smokes one for us.

Convenience Is Our Master

Does one not suspect that truth is a word?
So much for the diamond on your thumb.
I want to be roundelay about this.

Return to my suspicions.
Aroma, rhythm, skeptical tonality and
and ounce or less or more of that thing.

It's the thing we all know is among us.
It droops and sways and bubbles up us
to where our willing hearts obey and surrender.

The invisible is certainly invincible
should we care enough too fight it.
Why not let it be the thing we need
to make our heart beats matter?

Eternity

Zero to sixty in point one second or less
—c'est magnifique, non?
Buy the next creature you see
that can speak to you of its good luck.
The insect caught in amber
is a good example of undetermined fortune.
What's good for you could be hell for me.
The situation is not hopeless;
it has yet to be decided.

About the author

Lewis was born and raised in Providence and has been resident in the San Francisco Bay Area since 1959. He wrote his first poem in 1948 at age 11. In 1955 he shared authorship of a small chapbook called *two in you th* with his friend (and printer) Darrell Hyder. In 1961 some of his poetry was included in a bilingual anthology edited by Gregory Corso titled *Junge Amerikanische Lyrik* (which included many of the same poets Donald Allen selected to use in his anthology *The New American Poetry 1945-1960*). In the 1960s Lewis's poetry was published in Richard Duerden's *Rivoli Review*, Stan Persky's *Open Space* and in Bill Levy's *The Insect Trust Gazette* after which he discontinued submitting poems for publication in magazines. Since then he has had several limited edition chapbooks printed: *Algebra for Breakfast* (1986), *Panama Poems* (1992), *Travel* (1993), *OXO Poems* (2001), *MDCC* (2004), *25 Poems* (2004) and *20/20* (2007).

He writes: "While the results may not necessarily show it, I believe I mimic a process of finding poems which I think is mainly about listening and is exemplified by the masters Wallace Stevens ('Poetry must be irrational') and Jack Spicer ('A system of dreaming fake dreams'). Usually what I hear is hairy, routeless, hardly satisfying and tarred with mistakes. But anyway...."